W9-BGZ-442

Kofi

and

His

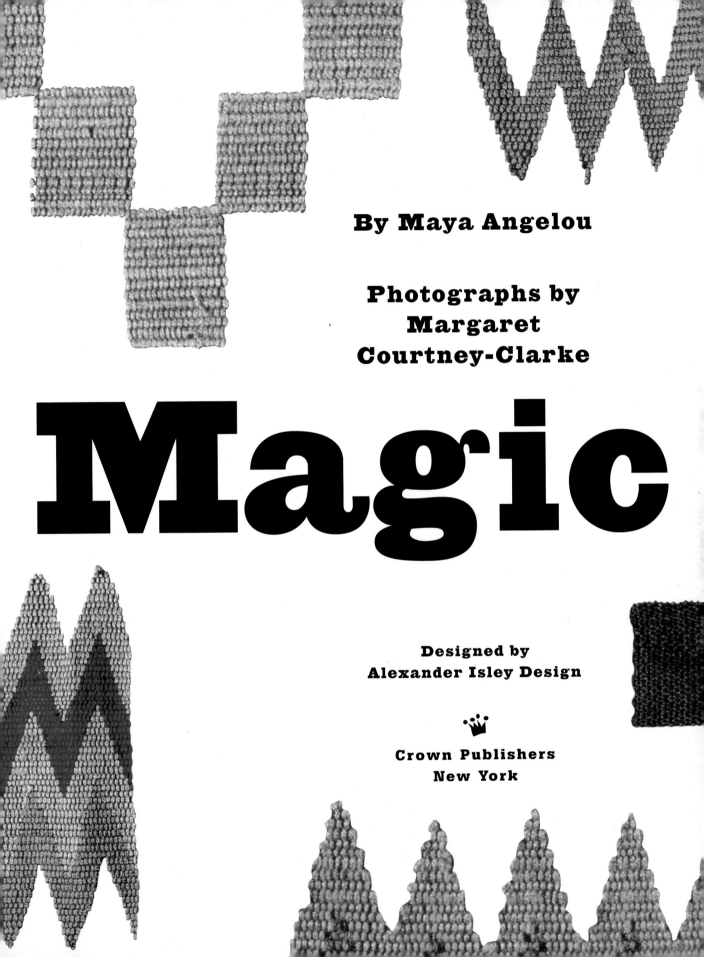

By Maya Angelou

Photographs by
Margaret
Courtney-Clarke

Magic

Designed by
Alexander Isley Design

♛

Crown Publishers
New York

Copyright © 1996 by Maya Angelou
and Margaret Courtney-Clarke

All rights reserved. No part of this book may be
reproduced or transmitted in any form or by any means,
electronic or mechanical, including photocopying,
recording, or by any information storage and retrieval
system, without permission in writing from the publisher.

Published by Crown Publishers, an imprint of
Random House Children's Books, a division
of Random House, Inc., New York.

Originally published in hardcover in 1996
by Clarkson N. Potter/Publishers.
First Crown edition March 2003

CROWN and colophon are trademarks
of Random House, Inc.

www.randomhouse.com/kids

Library of Congress Cataloging-in-Publication Data
Angelou, Maya.
Kofi and his magic / by Maya Angelou ; photographs by
Margaret Courtney-Clarke.
p. cm.
Summary: A young Ashanti boy describes some of
the wonders of his life in and around the West African
village of Bonwire.
1. Children, Ashanti—Social life and customs—Juvenile
literature. 2. Kente cloth—Ghana—Bonwire—Juvenile
literature. 3. Bonwire (Ghana)—Social life and customs—
Juvenile literature.
[1. Ashanti (African people). 2. Ghana—Social life and
customs.] I. Courtney-Clarke, Margaret, 1949- ill.
II. Title.
DT507.A54 1996   96-29210
966.7'004963385—dc20   CIP
AC

ISBN 0-375-82566-5 (trade pbk.)
ISBN 0-375-92566-X (lib. bdg.)

Printed in China

10 9 8 7 6 5 4 3 2 1

I dedicate my work in this
book to my late sister
Efua Sutherland and all
the children of Ghana who
were her children too.
— M.A.

For Emmanuel, Erik,
and the twins
Beatrice No. 1 and
Beatrice No. 2.
— M.C.-C.

Hi.

My name is Kofi, and I am a magician.

No, wait now...

My name is Kofi,
I live in West Africa,
the most beautiful
place in the whole
world, and I am
seven years old.

And I am a magician.

I live near the Ashanti golden stool, which everyone knows is pure magic.

The stool is made of gold and only the Ashanti king can sit on it. When he does, he becomes so powerful that everyone must obey his commands.

That's magic.

You may
think I'm
kidding
**when I
say I'm a
magician,**

but when I finish my story I'm sure you will believe me.

Okay, first I am, as I
said, Kofi, which means
I am a boy born on
Friday, and I am
a weaver. I weave
Kente cloth, the most
beautiful and richest
cloth in the world.

You may think I am not old enough to be a weaver,

but I began learning years ago when I was young.

I joined a class of boys learning to weave. The teacher tied threads to our toes and then we would move our feet a little like riding a bicycle. Just a little.

It was hard, but we had fun wiggling our toes, and I could make the threads behave.

But that's not why I am a magician.

My town is called Bonwire, and it is the most famous town in all the

world for Kente weaving.

I don't tell everyone, but I can do a magic thing and make

what I want to come true,   **come true.**

For example...I know Bonwire
is the best town in the world,
but sometimes I want to go to
other places...like the north
where people live in houses
different from ours, and wear
different clothes, and speak dif-
ferently, and eat different foods.

I also like to hear the
names of their towns,
Tamale, Sunyani, and
Bolgatanga.

So,

I sit down,
Close my eyes,
And open my
mind,

and I am on a bus, waving good-bye

to my friends in Bonwire.

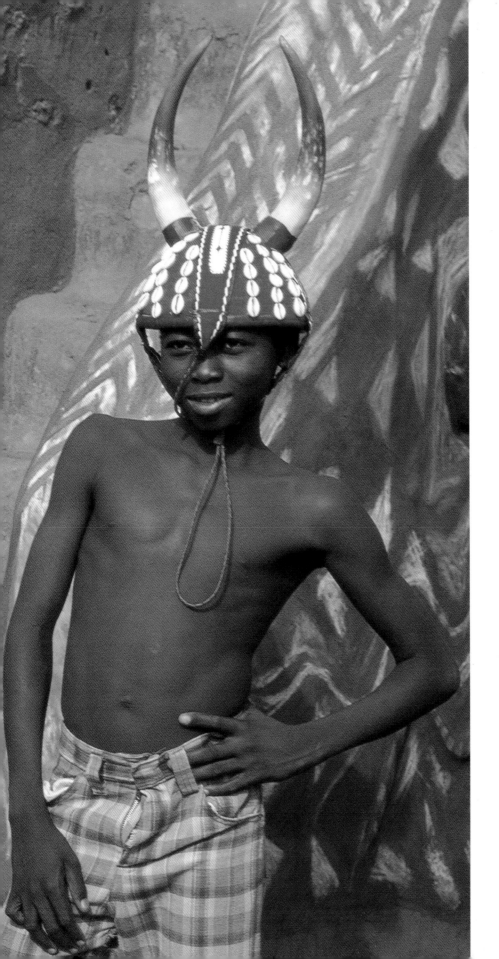

Then, suddenly, I am in the north.

Up here, no one weaves Kente, but they make other cloth. The boys wear hats made with horns and cowrie shells. If I wore a hat like that, I would feel very brave.

When I first see the northern
women painting their houses,
**I laugh because Ashanti
women don't do that.**

But, then I see how beautiful the
houses are when they are fin-
ished, and I think it would be
magical to live in a painted house.

The northern people like me.

They give me a smock like a big shirt to wear and let me

When I am ready
to go home,

stand with their wise old men.

I sit down,
Close my eyes,
Open my mind,

And I'm back in Bonwire going to school.

We carry our desks to write on

and stools to sit

on because most

of the time classes are outside.

During the rainy

season, we go

inside a building

to study.

Sometimes I get

bored and have

to use my magic.

I sit down,
Close my eyes,
Open my mind,

And I am at a festival called a **Durbar**. Every year at harvest time, **the people celebrate**. Powerful chiefs, some of whom are women priests, and wise men **put on their richest Kente and gold** and they are carried through the streets on palanquins **under beautiful umbrellas.**

Dancers and drummers
fill the roads.
With singers singing,
children shouting,
and the *thump*, *thump*
of the drums,

the noise is wonderful.

There is delicious food to eat everywhere.

I love the Durbar, but I do get tired, so

**I sit down,
Close my eyes,
Open my mind,**

**and I am
back home
in Bonwire
with my friend
Kojo who
doesn't laugh
very much.**

I decide to share my magic with Kojo.

I tell him we should go to the sea, and I say

Sit down,
Close your eyes,
Open your mind,

And...

I have to repeat myself many times, but at last we both

Sit down,
Close our eyes,
Open our minds,

and then we are at a lake so wide and blue that we become afraid.

But someone tells us that what we are looking at is not a lake, but the Atlantic Ocean.

It has a wonderful

smell and a wonderful

roar like a soft roll of

thunder in the raining

season, and the water

tastes salty.... After a

while, Kojo wants to

go home, so we

Sit down,
Close our eyes,
Open our minds,

And we are back in Bonwire.

I told you at first that I was a magician. Well, I have been thinking in my language, Ashanti, and you have been hearing me in English. So, I think you must be a magician too.

If you ever want to meet me, just

Sit down,
Close your eyes,
Open your mind,

and think about a friend you have in West Africa named Kofi.